This Journal is a gift
to a
grandfather that's
a pretty funny guy:

_____

_____

## Write a message to your grandfather:

I (We) love you because

Thank you for all you do.

Love,

# My grandfather is awesome because he:

- ☐ Tells the best worst jokes
- ☐ Tells the worst best jokes
- ☐ Gives the best tickles
- ☐ Gives the best snuggles
- ☐ Gives me cookies
- ☐ Gives me candy
- ☐ Gives the best hugs
- ☐ Takes me to the movies
- ☐ Takes me fishing
- ☐ Takes me shopping
- ☐ Takes me to dinner
- ☐ Takes me to the park
- ☐ Takes me on trips
- ☐ Takes me on walks
- ☐ Takes me to my games
- ☐ Reads with me
- ☐ Teaches me to fish
- ☐ Teaches me to fly a kite
- ☐ Tells me family stories
- ☐ Helps me with homework
- ☐ Helps me be the best I can be
- ☐ Makes me feel loved

**Okay Grandpa, enough of the mushy stuff, you start here:**

Tell us all of your jokes, puns, one-liners and tall tales. Make sure to keep them kid friendly!

My best bad joke is:

## My best poop joke is:

My best knock knock joke is:

## My best lame joke is:

## My best grandmother joke is:

## My best political joke is:

## My best animal joke is:

My best fart joke is:

## My best one-liner is:

## My best tall tale is:

## My best pull-my-finger joke is:

My best fishing joke is:

## Did you hear the one about?...

## My best golf joke is:

## When I was a kid:

Visit Meadow Road Books
for a list of more journals.

Visit the author at
SillyYaya.com
for a complete list of
children's books.

Follow the author and
Meadow Road Books
on social media @
Silly Yaya and Meadow Road Books
*Facebook
*Facebook Group/Grandparenting
Plain and Simple
*Instagram
*Twitter

©Meadow Road Books

Made in the USA
Middletown, DE
16 December 2019